PRAY IT 100 TIMES: FEAR NOT!

A PRAYER MANUAL

Cynthia E. J. Carter

i

PRAY IT 100 TIMES: FEAR NOT!

A PRAYER MANUAL

Cynthia E. J. Carter

Pray It 100 Times: Fear Not!

Unless otherwise indicated, all Scripture quotations are from the King James Version.

Contact Information
For information on how to get additional copies of the "Pray It 100 Times: Fear Not!" or other books and materials, please contact:

Cynthia Carter @ Virtuous Books
P. O. Box 23200
Houston, TX 77228-3200
Phone: (832) 409-4325

Email: cynthiaejcarter@att.net
Website: www.cynthiacarterministries.net or
www.wutsministries.org

Pray It 100 Times: Fear Not!

Acknowledgements

I am grateful for many family members and friends whom support the call of God on my life. I could never name them all. However, for the development and production of this book, I feel a deep sense of gratitude to:

- Most importantly, God Almighty who is the author and finisher of our faith who has called me and anointed me to write and preach the gospel of Jesus Christ.
- To the members of WUTS Ministries for their confidence and commitment to me as their Pastor. Words could never express how honored I am.
- To my daughter Ayasha Greene and Jacqueline Britton for proofreading and for excellent suggestions in editing the manuscript.
- To Johnny and Gloria Espinoza who embraced my ministry in intercession and financial support of this book.

Introduction

In the beginning, man feared nothing! Why? Because, God breathed His Holy Spirit into Adam for life and to teach him all things. He was perfectly created in God's image (Gen.1:27). God's image is perfect supremacy in heaven and earth; and God is love (Ps 24:1, I Jo. 4:8). God sat Adam down in the midst of an uncultivated world and declared to him, "have dominion" (Gen. 1:28). Adam readily began exploring the nature of the world and ascribing names accordingly. His love for God lead him to trust his God given ability to respond to his life's calling from God by faith. When the venomous serpent was before Adam for naming, there was not a flinch in his nature. Adam had no need for courage because the spirit of fear did not exist. His perfect love for God prevented fear from affecting his ability or decision to fulfill God's mandate for his life. However, man's disposition to fear changed the moment he separated himself from God through a sinful decision.

Adam's decision, known as the "Fall of Man", led to man's first encounter with fear. The Word of God records this event in Genesis 3:1-10:

> *(v1) Now the serpent was more subtil than any beast of the field which the LORD God had made. And he said unto the woman, Yea, hath God said, Ye shall not eat of every tree of the garden? (v2) And the woman said unto the serpent, We may eat of the fruit of the trees of the garden: (v3) But of the fruit of the tree*

which is in the midst of the garden, God hath said, Ye shall not eat of it, neither shall ye touch it, lest ye die. (v4) And the serpent said unto the woman, ye shall not surely die: (v5) For God doth know that in the day ye eat thereof, then your eyes shall be opened, and ye shall be as gods, knowing good and evil. (v6) And when the woman saw that the tree was good for food, and that it was pleasant to the eyes, and a tree to be desired to make one wise, she took of the fruit thereof, and did eat, and gave unto her husband with her; and he did eat. (v7) And the eyes of them both were opened, and they knew that they were naked; and they sewed fig leaves together, and made themselves aprons. (v8) And they heard the voice of the LORD God walking in the garden in the cool of the day: and Adam and his wife hid themselves from the presence of the LORD God amongst the trees of the garden. (v9) And the LORD God called unto Adam, and said unto him, Where art thou? (v10) And he said, I heard thy voice in the garden, and I was afraid, because I was naked; and I hid myself.

The subtleness of Satan, Eve voicing her opinion, and Adam not standing upright with his knowledge of God's command caused the reversal of the spirit of truth in the consciousness of man. The "one" sinful decision to eat of the "one and only" tree which God told him not to eat began the torment of evil and fear. Immediately, he and his wife are tormented by all evil forces of fear lurking outside of God's perfect love.

Pray It 100 Times: Fear Not!

Fear became an interference in Adam and Eve's once perfect relationship with God.

The spirit of fear causes the truth to have an adverse affect on Adam and Eve's decisions. Now Adam was misappropriating his decisions in response to God's presence. Instead of trusting the voice of God and the Holy Spirit of Truth that he had trusted before the fall, he fled from God's serenity to isolation in his sin. His God given dominion was shaken by the spirit of fear until he could no longer see himself as the image of God. He saw his nakedness and hid from the one who created the earth for him to have dominion over. The unholy spirit of fear then boasts itself against the knowledge of truth. Mankind has run from the presence of God and their destiny ever since. Let me share an example from my personal encounter with the spirit of fear:

Growing up with seven brothers in the country, I often played in the yard, walked the trails to church, to the house of friends or grandparents alone. Daily, I encountered snakes - big ones, little ones, poisonous and non-poisonous snakes. I lacked fear! The snakes went their way and I went mine. Until the age of 10, I walked home from Church on a Resurrection Sunday, my normal encounter with snakes occurred - this time there were two snakes. One was in the ditch. Causally, I picked up a rock and threw it at the snake and as countless times before, it slithered away.

Pray It 100 Times: Fear Not!

However, the second snake, as subtle in deception as the serpent in the Garden of Eden, lay to my right on the top of a fence in the pathway I had to cross. Like before, I picked up a rock, aimed at the snake and threw it believing it would slither away also. Stunned and in disbelief, this snake dropped to the ground and the chase began! I didn't know I could run so fast. Running, screaming for help, full of panic, not sure if I could make it to safety, I kept looking back to see how close it was to me. I felt it gaining on me... Finally, arriving within yards of my great grandparents' house where the family was having dinner I felt safety. Thank God the garden-hoe was handy. My step-dad and uncles wasted no time running to meet me and greet that snake with its final destiny – death! Still, long after that tormenting event, I remained plagued by the presence of snakes.

Irrational fear gripped me at the thought of seeing another snake. Satan's evil spirit tormented me with fear if I saw a snake on television or a magazine. If I saw one while walking to school, I would detour to the next street to get to the bus stop or wait for someone else to walk with me. My best friend had a python as a pet and I stop going to play because of it. The fear grew worse over the years – it carried over into my adulthood. Several times, a snake crawled to my front door – my neighbor, a woman like myself, killed one of the snakes with ease. I felt embarrassed that I could not kill the snake myself. I began to seek God, the Father for my deliverance.

Pray It 100 Times: Fear Not!

Now ready to confront fear, God revealed to my heart his powerful ability to restore dominion in the lives of His children. Genesis 3:15 is our restoration to being bold and courageous:

> And I will put enmity between you and the woman, And between your seed and her Seed; He shall **bruise** your head, And you shall **bruise** His heel."

How dare Satan keep tormenting God's people with his unholy spirit of fear! The promise of God is that we "shall bruise" the head of the serpent. Satan still boasts through serpentine spirits to perpetuate the spirit of fear against mankind. That second serpent reared its ugly head at me and chased after its death! I confronted that spirit at its point of entrance and picked up my God given right to have dominion over every area of my life.

Fear is at the root of all spiritual and physical stagnation to the God ordained destinies of people. Everyone, at some point, struggles or has struggled with fear. People are immobilized, tormented and trapped by limitations imposed through fear. I deem fear as one of Satan's greatest weapons. Until Christians recognize fear as an opposing force that threatens our very existence, and deliberately counter attack it with the Word of God, we will not fulfill our commission to have signs that follow our faith. If we desire to win this spiritual warfare on every level of life, we cannot afford to take the weapon of fear lightly!

God Perspective on Fear

God, does not take fear for granted. Let us look at God's instructions to Gideon concerning fear and his army:

> *Now therefore go to, proclaim in the ears of the people, saying, Whosoever is fearful and afraid, let him return and depart early from mount Gilead. And there returned of the people twenty and two thousand; and there remained ten thousand.*
>
> *Judges 7:3*

Did you catch that number? Out of "32,000" men in Gideon's army, "22,000" of them were fearful. Twenty-two thousand men were in a spiritual no-win situation with fear that could have taken their lives on the battlefield. God was not yet through with decreasing Gideon's army and dealing with fear on the battlefield. The following verse explains:

> *(v7) And the LORD said unto Gideon, by the three hundred men that lapped will I save you, and deliver the Midianites into thine hand: and let all the other people go every man unto his place.*

With a host of 32,000 men to back him up in the battle, Gideon would possess a reasonable amount of confidence that he could win the war. With 10,000 warriors, he perhaps had a fighting chance. But now,

Pray It 100 Times: Fear Not!

God appears to have decreased the odds of manpower in favor of the enemy's multitudes to Gideon's 300 men. Talking about a reason to fear in the natural flesh! Gideon is called to conquer a battle that he could not have possibly won without supernatural help from God.

By now Gideon, is shaken with fear. God instructed Gideon to go to the camp of his enemies to help him overcome his fear of failure and death. Essentially, God told Gideon to sneak up on his enemies, the Midianites, and listen to their conversation.

> *(v9) And it came to pass the same night, that the LORD said unto him, Arise, get thee down unto the host; for I have delivered it into thine hand.(v10) But if thou fear to go down, go thou with Phurah thy servant down to the host: (v11) And thou shalt hear what they say; and afterward shall thine hands be strengthened to go down unto the host. Then went he down with Phurah his servant unto the outside of the armed men that were in the host. (v12) And the Midianites and the Amalekites and all the children of the east lay along in the valley like grasshoppers for multitude; and their camels were without number, as the sand by the seaside for multitude. (v13) And when Gideon was come, behold, there was a man that told a dream unto his fellow, and said, Behold, I dreamed a dream, and, lo, a cake of barley bread tumbled into the host of Midian, and came unto a tent, and smote it that it fell, and*

overturned it, that the tent lay along. (v14) And his fellow answered and said, This is nothing else save the sword of Gideon the son of Joash, a man of Israel: for into his hand hath God delivered Midian, and all the host. (v15) And it was so, when Gideon heard the telling of the dream, and the interpretation thereof, that he worshipped, and returned into the host of Israel, and said, Arise; for the LORD hath delivered into your hand the host of Midian.

Judges 7:7, 9-15

God terrorized Gideon's enemies by way of their dreams. So much so, that they talked among themselves of the victory Gideon would have over them. At that point, Gideon leaped for joy and expelled all of his fears concerning the war.

The spirit of man must be fearless in order to envision victory over his enemies in battle. God took time to eliminate the fearful men from Gideon's army and he dealt with Gideon's fear as an individual and a leader. God recognizes fear as a defeating foe in the character of Christians when engaging in warfare of any kind. Therefore, just as he addressed Gideon's fears and commanded him with words of instructions, God commands us over and over again in His Word to stand up against fear. Fear is a trial of spiritual warfare and God has provided us an escape through his word. Most of all, we must "know" that it is God's battle. God will prove himself in a way that we cannot take the credit for His victory through us.

It's Elementary

During my early childhood school days, if a student acted out as the class clown or got caught doing something he or she should not be doing in the classroom, the teacher made the student write "100" times on the blackboard or on a sheet of paper, **"I will not..."** In addition to that, the student received an incomplete grade on the assignment due that day or was sent to detention. This was the teacher's way of reinforcing and embedding in the student's mind and spirit that he or she should not repeat the infraction. If the notion came up again, the student quickly dispelled it not wanting to reap the same or even greater consequences.

Finally, let me introduce you to an elementary, yet powerful, method of knowing, praying and hearing God's word as your personal command to victory over fear. It is a method that I use personally when encountering fear factors in my life.

By utilizing the method by faith in, *Pray It 100 Times: Fear Not!*, you will be able to acknowledge, learn and speak God's word over your life so that your spirit man will grow boldly and courageously to stand up in the power of the Holy Spirit. By standing up in God's power, you will win the battle over fear factors in your life! This book contains a list of One hundred scriptures, each one followed by a prayer. Simply read each scripture aloud and pray the prayer aloud over yourself by placing your name on the blank line in the prayer. Keep in mind the firm foundation that

Pray It 100 Times: Fear Not!

this spiritual exercise is built upon God's word through the following scriptures:

So then faith cometh by hearing, and hearing by the word of God. Roman 10:17

So shall my word be that goeth forth out of my mouth: it shall not return unto me void, but it shall accomplish that which I please, and it shall prosper in the thing whereto I sent it. Isaiah 55:11

Then said he unto me, Fear not, Daniel: for from the first day that thou didst set thine heart to understand, and to chasten thyself before thy God, thy words were heard, and I am come for thy words. Daniel 10:12

For the word of God is quick, and powerful, and sharper than any two edged sword, piercing even to the dividing asunder of soul and spirit, and of the joints and marrow, and is a discerner of the thoughts and intents of the heart. Hebrews 4:12

And that from a child thou hast known the holy scriptures, which are able to make thee wise unto salvation through faith which is in Christ Jesus. (v16) All scriptures is given by inspiration of God, and is profitable for doctrine, for reproof, for correction, for instruction in righteousness: (v17) That the man of God may be perfect, thoroughly furnished unto all good works. II Timothy 3:15-17

At this time, advance your attack against fear so that you may accomplish your God ordained destiny.

Pray It 100 Times: Fear Not!

1. After these things the word of the LORD came unto Abram in a vision, saying, Fear not, Abram: I am thy shield, and thy exceeding great reward. **Genesis 15:1**

Pray: The Word of the Lord has come to me, _____, saying, Fear not, _____: I am thy shield and your exceeding great reward.

2. And God heard the voice of the lad; and the angel of God called to Hagar out of heaven, and said unto her, what alieth thee Hagar? Fear not; for God hath heard the voice of the lad where he is. **Genesis 21:17**

Pray: What is bothering you, _____? Fear Not, _____. The Lord will speak to you concerning your children and your future.

3. And the LORD appeared unto him the same night, and said, I am the God of Abraham thy father: fear not, for I am with thee, and will bless thee, and multiply thy seed for my servant Abraham's sake. **Genesis 26:24**

Pray: Fear not, _____, for the Lord is with you, and will bless you, and multiply thy seed for His promise sake to your spiritual father and His servant, Abraham.

4. And it came to pass, when she was in hard labour, that the midwife said unto her, Fear Not; thou shalt have this son also. **Genesis 35:17**

Pray: Fear not, _____, you shall have this fulfillment of promises that your children come forth to their anointed destiny.

5. And he said, Peace be to you, fear not: your God, and the God of your father, hath given you treasure in your sacks: I had your money. And he brought Simeon out unto them. **Genesis 43:23**

Pray: Peace be to you _____, fear not: your God, and the God of your spiritual father will give you treasure in your wallet, purse, and bank accounts.

6. And he said, I am God, the God of thy father: fear not to go down into Egypt: for I will there make of thee a great nation. **Genesis 46:3**

Pray: And God's word says unto me, _____, I am God, the God of thy father: Fear not, _____, to go out and face the world: For I will make of you a great success.

7. And Joseph said unto them, Fear not: for am I in the place of God? **Genesis 50:19**

Pray: Fear not, _____, there is no one in the place of God over your life. Therefore, He is in control of your enemies also.

8. Now therefore fear ye not: I will nourish you, and your little ones. And he comforted them, and spake kindly unto them. **Genesis 50:21**

Pray: Fear not, _____, The Lord will nourish you, and your little ones. The Lord will comfort you, _____, and speak kind words to lead you through life.

9. And Moses said unto the people, Fear ye not, stand still, and see the salvation of the LORD, which he will show to you today; you shall see them again no more forever. The Lord shall fight for you, and you shall hold your peace. **Exodus 14:13-14**

Pray: Fear not, _____, stand still, and see the salvation of the Lord, which he will show to you today; you will not have to keep facing the same enemy. The Lord shall fight for you, _____, and you shall hold your peace.

10. And Moses said unto the people, Fear not: for God is come to prove you, and that his fear may be before your faces, that you sin not. **Exodus 20:20**

Pray: Fear not, _____, for God is come to test you and establish you in understanding holy fear before your face, that you sin not.

11. If the LORD delight in us, then he will bring us into this land and give it us; a land which floweth with milk and honey. Only rebel not you against the LORD, neither fear you the people of the land; for they are bread for us: their defense is departed from them, and the LORD is with us: fear them not. *Numbers 14:8-9*

Pray: The Lord will delight in you, _____, and bring you into land that flows with blessing. Rebel not, _____, against the Lord neither fear your enemies in the world; for they are a source of bread for you. They have no defense against the Lord that is with you. Fear them not _____.

12. And the Lord said unto Moses, Fear him not: for I have delivered him into thy hand, and all his people, and his land; and thou shalt do to him as thou didst unto Sihon king of the Amorites, which dwelt at Heshbon. **Numbers 21:34**

Pray: And the Lord said unto me, _____, Fear not the control of your enemy; for I have delivered him into your hands, and anyone who stands with him, and his land: and you shall have victory over your enemies.

13. Behold, the LORD thy God has set the land before thee: go up and possess it, as the LORD God of thy fathers has said unto thee; fear not, neither be discouraged. **Deuteronomy 1:21**

Pray: Behold, _____, the Lord, your God has set the land before you: go up and possess it, as the Lord God of your spiritual fathers has said unto you; fear not, _____, neither be discouraged.

14. And the Lord said unto me, Fear him not: for I will deliver him, and all his people, and his land, into thy hand; and thou shalt do unto him as thou didst unto Sihon king of the Amorites, which dwelt at Heshbon. **Deuteronomy 3:2**

Pray: And the Lord said unto me again, _____, Fear not your enemy; for I have delivered him into your hand, and all the people that stand with him, and you will be able to prosper from his land: and you shall have victory over your enemies.

15. Ye shall not fear them: for the LORD your God he shall fight for you. **Deuteronomy 3:22**

Pray: You, _____, shall not fear people for the Lord your God shall fight for you.

16. And shall say unto them, Hear, O Israel, Ye approach this day unto battle against your enemies: Let not your hearts faint, fear not, and do not tremble, neither be ye terrified because of them; For the LORD your God is he that goeth with you, to fight for you against your enemies, to save you. **Deuteronomy 20:3-4**

Pray: The Lord's Word says unto me, Hear, O, _____, You approach this day unto battle against your enemies: Let not your heart faint, fear not, _____, and do not tremble _____, neither be terrified _____, because of them. For the Lord your God is he that goes with you to fight for you, _____ against your enemies, to save you.

17. Be strong and of good courage, Fear not, nor be afraid of them: for the LORD thy God, he it is that doth go with thee; he will not fail thee, nor forsake thee. **Deuteronomy 31:6**

Pray: Be strong and of good courage, _____. Fear not _____, nor be afraid of enemies or your circumstances: for the Lord thy God, He is the one that goes with you. He will not fail you, _____, nor forsake you.

18. And the LORD, he it is that doth go before thee; he will be with thee, he will not fail thee, neither forsake thee: fear not, neither be dismayed. **Deuteronomy 31:8**

Pray: The Lord, Himself, goes before you, _____: he will be with you, _____everywhere you go. He will not fail you, _____, neither will he forsake you; fear not, _____ and do not let disappointment set in.

19. And the LORD said unto Joshua, Fear not, neither be thou dismayed: take all the people of war with thee, and arise, go up to Ai: see, I have given into thy hand the king of Ai, and his people, and his city, and his land. **Joshua 8:1**

Pray: And the LORD said unto me, _____, Fear not, neither be distraught: gather with all the people of God and arise in prayer. I have given into your hands, _____, the ability to possess victory over the leader of your enemies and his people, and his city, and his land.

20. And the LORD said unto Joshua, Fear them not: for I have delivered them into thine hand; there

shall not a man of them stand before thee.
Joshua 10:8.

Pray: And the LORD said unto me, _____, Fear no enemy: for I have delivered them into your hand; there shall not a man of them stand before you.

21. And Joshua said to them, Fear not, nor be dismayed, be strong and of good courage: for thus shall the LORD do to all your enemies against whom ye fight. **Joshua 10:25**

Pray: Fear not, _____, nor be dismayed, be strong and of good courage_____: for the Lord will fight your enemies against whom you fight against for you.

22. And Jael went out to meet Sisera, and said unto him, Turn in, my Lord, turn in to me; fear not. And when he had turned in unto her into the tent, she covered him with a mantle. (v21) Then Jael, Heber's wife took a nail of the tent, and took an hammer in her hand, and went softly unto him, and smote the nail into his temples, and fasted it into the ground: for he was fast asleep and weary. So he died. **Judges 4:18, 21.**

Pray: I, _____, will not fear the host of principalities that come up against my life. I, _____, will smite the head of every evil force that comes up against me and claim victory over the enemy through the nail scarred hands of Jesus. Every weapon formed against me will die out of my life.

23. And I said unto you, I am the LORD your God; fear not the gods of the Amorites in whose land ye dwell: but ye have not obeyed my voice. **Judges 6:10.**

Pray: And the Lord has said unto me, _____, I am the Lord your God; fear not, _____, those who appear to have ungodly rule over your life as gods of this world. But, _____, obey the voice of God.

24. And the LORD said unto him, Peace be unto thee; fear not: thou shalt not die. **Judges 6:23.**

Pray: And the Lord said unto me, _____, fear not. You, _____, shall not die.

25. And now, my daughter, fear not: I will do to thee all that thou requirest: for all the city of my people doth know that thou are a virtuous woman. **Ruth 3:11.**

Pray: And now, _____, my child, fear not. I will give you the desire of your heart in as much you have walked before me with a honorable spirit.

26. And about the time of her death the women that stood by her said unto her, Fear not: for thou hast born a son. But she answered not, neither did she regard it. **I Samuel 4:20**.

Pray: Even in the face of spiritual or physical death I, _____, will not fear! The Lord will cause my seed to be strong and healthy that they may carry on the work of His ministry.

27. And Samuel said unto the people, Fear not: ye have done all this wickedness: yet turn not aside from following the LORD, but serve the LORD with all your heart. **I Samuel 12:20**.

Pray: Though I, _____, have sinned against God, I will not fear to go to Him for mercy nor will I, _____, turn away from serving Him with all of my heart.

28. Abide thou with me, fear not: for he that seeketh my life seeketh thy life: but with me thou shalt be in safeguard. **I Samuel 22:23**.

Pray: Abide with the Lord, _____, and fear not. Those that seek your life will have to face the safeguard of the Lord.

29. And he said unto him, Fear not: for the band of Saul my father shall not find thee; and thou shalt be king over Israel, and I shall be next unto thee;

and that also Saul my father knoweth.   **I Samuel 23:17.**

Pray: Fear not, _____, the Lord will raise up a safe haven for you through the seed of your enemies. The love of God through you, _____, will cause your enemy's seed to serve and bless you.

30. And David said unto him, Fear not: for I will surely show thee kindness for Jonathan thy father's sake, and will restore thee all the land of Saul thy father; and thou shalt eat bread at my table continually. **II Samuel 9:7.**

Pray: Fear not, _____, the Lord will raise you up to restore the land to righteousness. Even your enemy's seed will be converted and eat the bread of life from your table.

31. But Absalom pressed him, that he let Amnon and all the king's sons go with him. Now Absalom had commanded his servants, saying, Mark ye now when Amnon's heart is merry with wine, and when I say unto you, Smite Amnon; then kill him, fear not: have not I commanded you? Be courageous, and be valiant.   **II Samuel 13:27-28.**

Pray: Fear not, _____, but wait on the Lord. The Lord will cause vengeance to overtake your enemies. Be courageous and be valiant, _____, in the face of fear.

32. And Elijah said unto her, Fear not; go and do as thou hast said: but make me thereof a little cake first, and bring it unto me, and after make for thee and for thy son. **I Kings 17:13.**

Pray: Fear not, _____, to provide for the man or woman of God out of your lack. The prophecy of provisional blessing shall overtake you, _____, and shall not fail in the time of your need.

33. And he answered, Fear not: for they that be with us are more than they that be with them. And Elisha prayed, and said, LORD, I pray thee, open his eyes, that he may see, And the LORD opened the eyes of the young man; and he saw: and, behold, the mountain was full of horses and chariots of fire round about Elisha. **II Kings 6:16-17.**

Pray: Fear not, _____, when a host of principalities come up against you. The Lord will open your spiritual eyes _____ to see and know that He has provided an angelical host to protect and serve you.

34. With whom the LORD had made a covenant, and charged them, saying, Ye shall not fear other gods, nor bow yourselves to them, nor serve them, nor sacrifice to them. **II Kings 17:35.**

Pray: Fear not, _____. Do not enter in to contracts with evildoers that present themselves as gods. Do not fear retaliation from your enemies, nor serve or sacrifice your blessing to them because your covenant with God, _____, is greater.

35. And the statues, and the ordinances, and the law, and the commandment, which he wrote for you, ye shall observe to do for evermore; and ye shall not fear other gods. **II Kings 17:37.**

Pray: I, _____, will apply every concept and law of God's word to my life's situation as long as I live; and I will not fear to stand against principles that boast against the knowledge of God.

36. And the covenant that I have made with you ye shall not forget; neither shall ye fear other gods. **II Kings 17:38.**

Pray: Fear not, _____, the Lord is in covenant with you. There is no god greater than your God. So do not fear!

37. And Gedaliah sware to them, and to their men, and said unto them, Fear not to be the servants of the Chaldees: dwell in the land and serve the king of Babylon; and it shall be well with you. **II Kings 25:24.**

Pray It 100 Times: Fear Not!

Pray: _____, do not make false promises to your enemies. Let your yes be yes and your no be no. The Lord will fight your battles for you.

38. And David said to Solomon his son, Be strong and of good courage, and do it: fear not, nor be dismayed: for the LORD God, even my God, will be with thee; he will not fail thee, nor forsake thee, until thou hast finished all the work for the service of the house of the LORD. **I Chronicles 28:20.**

Pray: Be strong and of good courage, _____, and perform your assigned task from the Lord. Fear not failure, _____, nor be dismayed for the Lord God will be with you. He will not fail you or forsake you. You shall finish all the work God has assigned you for the service of the house of the Lord.

39. Ye shall not need to fight in this battle: set yourselves, stand ye still, and see the salvation of the LORD with you, nor be dismayed; tomorrow go out against them: for the LORD will be with you. **II Chronicles 20:17.**

Pray: _____, you will not have to fight in the battle you are going through right now. Fortify yourself, _____, and stand still, and watch to see God's salvation over you. Don't be weary, _____, but face the trial head on and the Lord is going to see you through.

40. Yea, though I walk through the valley of the shadow of death, I will fear no evil: for thou art with me; thy rod and thy staff they comfort me. **Psalms 23:4.**

Pray: Though I, _____, walk through the valley of the shadow of death, I, _____, will fear no evil because the Lord, my God is with me. With His rod of iron to protect and staff to correct me, the Father, Son and Holy Spirit will comfort me.

41. The LORD is my light and my salvation; whom shall I fear? The LORD is the strength of my life; of whom shall I be afraid? **Psalms 27:1.**

Pray: The Lord is my light and my salvation; whom shall I, _____, fear? The Lord is the strength of my life; of whom shall I, _____, be afraid?

42. Though an host should encamp against me, my heart shall not fear: though war should rise against me, in this will I be confident. **Psalms 27:3.**

Pray: Though an host of trails should encamp against me, _____, my heart shall not fear. Battles in warfare may come and go against me but I, _____, will be confident in my God.

43.I sought the LORD, and he heard me, and delivered me from all my fears. **Psalms 34: 4.**

Pray: I, _____, will seek the Lord and He will hear me and deliver me, _____, from all my fears.

44.In God I will praise his word, in God I have put my trust; I will not fear what flesh can do unto me. **Psalms 56:4.**

Pray: I, _____, will praise God for His word and put all of my trust in Him. I will not fear my flesh or what the flesh of another can do unto me because the Word of God will lead me,_____, in the way of peace.

45.Hear my voice, O God, in my prayer: preserve my life from fear of the enemy. **Psalms 64:1**

Pray: I, _____, cry unto you, O God, with my voice in prayer. Hear me, _____, and preserve my life from fear of enemies.

46.Praise ye the LORD. Blessed is the man that feareth the LORD, that delighteth greatly in his commandments. **Psalms 112:1**

Pray: I, _____, will praise the Lord! I, _____, am blessed of the Lord because I walk in great admiration and respect of Him and delight myself in His laws.

47. The LORD is on my side; I will not fear: what can man do unto me? **Psalms 118:6.**

Pray: The Lord is on my side. I, _____, will not fear what man can do to me.

48. Blessed is every one that feareth the LORD; that walketh in his ways. **Psalms 128:1.**

Pray: Blessed am I, _____, because I fear the Lord and seek continually to walk in His ways.

49. It is good that thou shouldest take hold of this; yea, also from this withdraw not thine hand: for he that feareth God shall come forth of them all. **Ecclesiastes 7:18.**

Pray: It is good that I, _____, should take hold of this method of praying and increase my strength in the word of God. I, _____, will not withdraw myself from its meditation and application in my life. If I walk in the fear and admiration of God, I will come forth out of every trial.

50. And say unto him, Take heed, and be quiet; fear not, neither be fainthearted for the two tails of these smoking firebrands, for the fierce anger of Rezin with Syria, and of the son of Remaliah. **Isaiah 7:4.**

Pray: I, _____, will take heed to the word of God to be quiet and fear not. Neither will I, _____, be fainthearted for the double troubles that come after me like smoking firebrands. The anger of demonic forces will flee from me because of the Greatness of my God.

51. Say ye not, A confederacy, to all them to whom this people shall say, A confederacy; neither fear ye their fear, nor be afraid. **Isaiah 8:12.**

Pray: I, _____, will not acknowledge a group of enemies as being more powerful than the God that is within me. Neither will I, _____, confess fear of them nor embrace their fears as my own.

52. Say to them that are of a fearful heart, Be strong, and fear not: behold, your God will come with vengeance, even God with a recompense; he will come and save you. **Isaiah 35:4.**

Pray: When I, _____, am fearful of heart, I will say to myself, be strong and fear not! God will avenge me and compensate me with blessings. He will come and save me.

53. Fear thou not; for I am with thee: be not dismayed; for I am thy God: I will strengthen thee; yea, I will help thee; yea, I will uphold thee with the right hand of my righteousness. **Isaiah 41:10.**

Pray: Fear not, _____, I am with you. Do not be disappointed for I am your God. I will strengthen you, _____, Yes I will! I, the Lord, your God, will uphold you with the right hand of my righteousness.

54. For I the LORD thy God will hold thy right hand, saying unto thee, Fear not; I will help thee. **Isaiah 41:13.**

Pray: I, _____, will hear the voice of God as He speaks to me, _____, through his word saying He will hold my right hand and help me with every trial. Fear not, _____.

55. Fear not, thou worm Jacob, and ye men of Israel; I will help thee, saith the Lord, and thy redeemer, the Holy One of Israel. **Isaiah 41:14.**

Pray: Fear not, _____, you are a caterpillar changing from your old image into a new creature in Christ. I will help you, says the Lord, your Redeemer and Holy One of Israel.

56. But now thus saith the LORD that created thee, O Jacob, and he that formed thee, O Israel, Fear not: for I have redeemed thee, I have called thee by thy name; thou art mine. **Isaiah 43:1.**

Pray: But now, _____, thus saith the Lord that created you, _____, and formed you in your mother's womb, Fear not! For the Lord have redeemed you and called you by your name, _____. You are the Lord's child.

57. Fear not: for I am with thee: I will bring thy seed from the east, and gather thee from the west; I will say to the north, Give up; and to the south, Keep not back: bring my sons from far, and my daughters from the ends of the earth; Even everyone that is called by my name: for I have created him for my glory, I have formed him; yea, I have made him. **Isaiah 43:5-7.**

Pray: Fear not, _____, for I am with you. I (God) will bring your children from the north, south, east and west. I will command salvation over your sons and daughters even if they run to the ends of the earth because I have created them for my glory. I formed your children, _____, and know where they are and what they need.

58. Thus saith the LORD that made thee, and formed thee from the womb, which will help thee; Fear not, O Jacob, my servant; and thou, Jesurun, whom I have chosen. **Isaiah 44:2.**

Pray: It is the Lord who has made you, _____, and formed you in the womb. He will help you through every trial of life. Fear not,

_____, you are my servant, a chosen seed that will bless my kingdom.

59. Fear ye not, neither be afraid: have not I told thee from that time, and have declared it? Ye are even my witnesses. Is there a God beside me? Yea, there is no God; I know not any. **Isaiah 44:8.**

Pray: Fear not, _____. You don't have to be afraid. Haven't I, the Lord, declared to you from the beginning of your walk with me that there is no other God besides me? I am your God, _____, and there is not another god greater than I.

60. Hearken unto me, ye that know righteousness, the people in whose heart is my law; fear ye not the reproach of men, neither be ye afraid of their revilings. **Isaiah 51:7.**

Pray: Listen to the words of God, _____, because you know what is righteous. Live the principles of the Word that He has written in your heart. Fear not, _____, the reproach of men and don't be afraid of their insults.

61. Fear not; for thou shalt not be ashamed: neither be thou confounded; for thou shalt not be put to shame: for thou shalt forget the shame of thy youth, and shalt not remember the reproach of thy widowhood any more. **Isaiah 54:4.**

Pray: Fear not, _____, for you shall not be ashamed. Don't allow yourself, _____, to be bewildered by your circumstances. You shall not be put to utter shame. I, God, will cause you to forget the shameful mistakes of your youth and I will not remember your sin anymore.

62. In righteousness shalt thou be established: thou shalt be far from oppression; for thou shalt not fear: and from terror; for it shall not come near thee. **Isaiah 54:14.**

Pray: In righteousness, _____, you shall be established. Don't allow fear to oppress you or cause terror in your life. I will keep you in peace.

63. And I will set up shepherds over them which shall feed them: and they shall fear no more, nor be dismayed, neither shall they be lacking, saith the LORD. **Jeremiah 23:4.**

Pray: I, _____, will know the good shepherds that God has ordained to feed me. I, _____, shall not fear or be confused in spiritual matters. I, _____, shall lack no good thing in the Lord.

64. Therefore fear thou not, O my servant Jacob, saith the LORD; neither be dismayed, O Israel: for, lo, I will save thee from afar, and thy seed from the land of their captivity; and Jacob shall return, and

shall be in rest, and be quiet, and none shall make him afraid. **Jeremiah 30:10.**

Pray: Fear not, _____. Do not let things get the better of you. You are a blessed and chosen seed of life and I, God, will bring both you and your seed out of every captivity. So rest and be quiet, _____, there is no one that can overcome your God with fear!

65. But fear not thou, O my servant Jacob, and be not dismayed, O Israel: for, behold, I will save thee from afar off, and thy seed from the land of their captivity; and Jacob shall return, and be in rest and at ease, and none shall make him afraid. **Jeremiah 46:27.**

Pray: Again I, the Lord, admonish you, _____, Fear not! Do not let things get the better of you. You, _____, are seed of my righteousness. I have chosen you and will bring both you and your children out of every captivity. So rest, _____ and be quiet. There is no one that can overcome your God with fear!

66. Fear thou not, O Jacob my servant, saith the LORD: for I am with thee; for I will make a full end of all the nations whither I have driven thee: but I will not make a full end of thee, but correct thee in measure; yet will I not leave thee wholly unpunished. **Jeremiah 46:28.**

Pray: Fear not my servant, _____. I, the Lord, am with you. The enemy's territory that polluted you, _____, with sin shall come to an end but I will correct you, _____, in measures through enough punishment to instill appreciation for my love and my instructions as a parent who loves His child.

67. Thou drewest near in the day that I called upon thee: thou saidst, Fear not. **Lamentations 3:57.**

Pray: I, _____, will not fear to draw near to God because as I, _____, call out to Him, He will draw near to me.

68. As an adamant harder than flint have I made thy forehead: fear them not, neither be dismayed at their looks, though they be a rebellious house. **Ezekiel 3:9.**

Pray: _____, do not consider the boasting looks on the face of those who are rebellious of my word with fear. I, the Lord, will instill boldness, courage and wisdom within you, _____, which shall shine in your face to blind your enemies.

69. Then said he unto me, Fear not, Daniel: for from the first day that thou didst set thine heart to understand, and to chasten thyself before thy God, thy words were heard, and I am come for thy words. **Daniel 10:12.**

Pray: _____, from the first day that you desired understanding and sacrificed yourself in prayer before God, your petition were heard. The angelical host presents your prayers, _____, before me, God.

70. And said, O man greatly beloved, fear not: peace be unto thee, be strong, yea, be strong. And when he had spoken unto me, I was strengthened, and said, Let my lord speak; for thou hast strengthened me. **Daniel 10:19.**

Pray: Peace is unto you O, _____. You are greatly beloved of God, fear not. Be strong! Again, Be strong! Let the word of God speak to you, _____, and be strengthened.

71. Fear not, O land; be glad and rejoice: for the LORD will do great things. **Joel 2:21.**

Pray: Be glad, _____, and rejoice in the truth! Fear is not of God. The Lord will do great things in your life _____.

72. In that day it shall be said to Jerusalem, fear thou not: and to Zion, Let not thine hands be slack. **Zephaniah 3:16.**

Pray: You, _____, are my child just as Jerusalem is the apple of my eyes. Just as I have heard my children cry out of Zion, so shall I hear your cries for help. Therefore, keep applying yourself, _____, to the vision that is set before you.

73. According to the word that I covenanted with you when ye came out of Egypt, so my spirit remaineth among you: fear ye not. **Haggai 2:5.**

Pray: According to the word of God that He has covenanted with me, _____, when I came out of the world, His Spirit will remain with me and I shall not fear this life.

74. And it shall come to pass, that as ye were a curse among the heathen, O house of Judah, and house of Israel; so will I save you, and ye shall be a blessing: fear not, but let your hands be strong. **Zechariah 8:13.**

Pray: It will come to pass, _____, that just as you acted and fulfilled the lust of your flesh when you were in the world, your praise, _____, and attendance to the house of God will save you. And you, _____, shall be a blessing to all you encounter. Fear not, _____, continue to learn and do whatever your hands find to do in the work of the Lord.

75. So again have I thought in these days to do well unto Jerusalem and to the house of Judah: fear ye not. **Zechariah 8:15.**

Pray: I, _____, will remain in the house of God among His people. His praises shall continually be in my mouth. I, _____, shall not walk in fear.

76. But while he thought on these things, behold, the angel of the Lord appeared unto him in a dream, saying, Joseph, thou son of David, fear not to take unto thee Mary thy wife: for that which is conceived in her is of the Holy Ghost. **Matthew 1:20.**

Pray: I, _____, have continual concerns towards my spouse to be but I will trust in the Lord to speak to me in a way that I understand and know that it is He, God, who speaks to me. Therefore I, _____, will not fear because the Holy Ghost is in control and will guide me in the way of truth and His good pleasure.

77. Fear them not therefore: for there is nothing covered, that shall not be revealed; and hid, that shall not be known. **Matthew 10:26.**

Pray: Do not take into account the weapons that have formed against you, _____, by others. There is nothing covered that shall not be revealed. The truth shall come out about every wicked scheme that is devised by others against you.

78. And fear not them which kill the body, but are not able to kill the soul: but rather fear him which is able to destroy both soul and body in hell. **Matthew 10:28.**

Pray It 100 Times: Fear Not!

Pray: _____, fear not those who may be able to take your life. Possess a holy fear of God, _____, who will destroy the body and soul of unbelievers in hell.

79. Fear ye not therefore, ye are of more value than many sparrows. **Matthew 10:31.**

Pray: _____, fear not! God watches over every sparrow's needs. You, _____, are much more important to Him.

80. And the angel answered and said unto the women, Fear not ye: for I know that ye seek Jesus, which was crucified. **Matthew 28:5.**

Pray: The messengers of the Lord, _____, yes, even angels will strengthen you, _____, and give you instructions from the word of God. Do not seek answers from the dead. _____, fear not, Jesus is alive!

81. But the angel said unto him, Fear not, Zacharias: for thy prayer is heard: and thy wife Elisabeth shall bear thee a son, and thou shalt call his name John. **Luke 1:13.**

Pray: The word of God speaks to me, _____, as did the angel prophecy to God's people. My prayers are heard and every good ministry that God has for me, _____, has been identified and shall come to pass.

82. And the angel said unto her, Fear not, Mary: for thou hast found favour with God. **Luke 1:30.**

Pray: Fear not, _____, you have found favor with God.

83. And the angel said unto them, Fear not: for, behold, I bring you good tidings of great joy, which shall be to all people. **Luke 2:10.**

Pray: Fear not, _____, hear the good tiding of great joy through the word of God. Your joy, _____, shall all the people see and be blessed.

84. And so was also James, and John, the sons of Zebedee, which were partners with Simon. And Jesus said unto Simon, Fear not; from henceforth thou shalt catch men. **Luke 5:10.**

Pray: _____, you shall be named among the disciples. From hence forth, _____, you shall evangelize to win the souls of men.

85. But when Jesus heard it, he answered him, saying, Fear not: believe only, and she shall be made whole. **Luke 8:50.**

Pray: Jesus has said, Fear not, _____, only believe and you will be made whole of any infirmity.

86. But even the very hairs of your head are all numbered. Fear not therefore: ye are of more value than many sparrows. **Luke 12:7.**

Pray: Again, _____, you are more valuable than the sparrows I watch over every minute. The very hairs on your head, _____, are numbered. I, the Lord have not forgotten about you. Fear not!

87. Fear not, daughter of Sion: behold, thy King cometh, sitting on an ass's colt. **John 12:15.**

Pray: Fear not, _____. Your King has already come to you in humble fashion. He has heard your cry for mercy.

88. Saying, Fear not, Paul; thou must be brought before Caesar: and, lo, God hath given thee all them that sail with thee. **Acts 27:24.**

Pray: Fear not death, _____. Your ministry assignment has to be fulfilled. The Lord will save others out of the storms of life with you.

89. For ye have not received the spirit of bondage again to fear; but ye have received the Spirit of adoption, whereby we cry, Abba, Father. **Romans 8:15.**

Pray: For you, _____, have not received the spirit of bondage again to fear. But,

_____, you have received the Spirit of adoption in to the family of God and have the right to cry, as His children cry, "Our Father" in the time of need.

90. Having therefore these promises, dearly beloved, let us cleanse ourselves from all filthiness of the flesh and spirit, perfecting holiness in the fear of God. **II Corinthians 7:1.**

Pray: You have the promises of God, dearly beloved _____. With those promises in mind, cleanse yourself, _____, from all filthiness of the flesh and spirit, perfecting holiness in the fear of God.

91. And many of the brethren in the Lord, waxing confident by my bonds, are much more bold to speak the word without fear. **Phillipians 1:14.**

Pray: I, _____, will grow strong in the Lord and will declare the word of God in boldness and without fear.

92. For God hath not given us the spirit of fear; but of power, and of love, and of a sound mind. **II Timothy 1:7**

Pray: God has not given me, _____, the spirit of fear but of power, love and a sound mind.

93. So that we may boldly say, The Lord is my helper, and I will not fear what man shall do unto me. **Hebrews 13:6.**

Pray: I, _____, will boldly declare that the Lord is my helper and I will not fear what man shall do unto me.

94. There is no fear in love; but perfect love casteth out fear: because fear hath torment. He that feareth is not made perfect in love. **I John 4:18.**

Pray: There is no fear in love, _____. The perfect love of God cast out fear, which has torment. If you fear, _____, you have not allowed yourself to be perfected in love. Fear not!

95. And when I saw him, I fell at his feet as dead. And he laid his right hand upon me, saying unto me, Fear not; I am the first and the last. **Revelation 1:17.**

Pray: I, _____, will not fear the revelation of the Lord. Nor will I faint at His correction. The Lord's right hand is upon me, _____, to strengthen me. I will not fear because He is the first and the last authority of my life.

96. Fear none of those things which thou shalt suffer: behold, the devil shall cast some of you into prison, that ye may be tried; and ye shall have tribulation ten days: be thou faithful unto death,

and I will give thee a crown of life. **Revelation 2:10.**

Pray: Fear none of those things, _____, which you shall suffer. The devil will try you with all kinds of bondages. Though you should have tribulations that last for days, be faithful until the death of sin occurs and I, the Lord, will give you, _____, a crown of life.

97. That thou mightest fear the LORD thy God, to keep all his statues and his commandments, which I command thee, thou, and thy son, and thy son's son, all the days of thy life; and that thy days may be prolonged. **Deuteronomy 6:2.**

Pray: That you, _____, walk and keep all the principles written in the word of God and teach your children to do so. Your seed, _____, grandchildren and great grandchildren will live a fruitful and long life.

98. Thou shalt fear the LORD thy God, and serve him, and shalt swear by his name. Ye shall not go after other gods, of the gods of the people which are round about you. **Deuteronomy 6:13-14.**

Pray: _____, there are many kinds of gods around you. Do not run after vain treasures, authority that exalt itself against the knowledge of God, or habits that control your life as other do. Walk in the admiration and reverence of God to serve him with all your heart and you will be able to use the power of His name.

99. And the LORD commanded us to do all these statues, to fear the LORD our God, for our good always, that he might preserve us alive, as it is at this day. **Deuteronomy 6:24.**

Pray: And the Lord commands me, _____, to walk in His laws always with a holy fear. As I, _____, hide His word in my heart and delight to live according to it, God will preserve my life.

100. Therefore thou shalt keep the commandments of the LORD thy God, to walk in his ways, and to fear him. **Deuteronomy 8:6.**

Pray: _____, you shall always keep the commandments of the Lord your God, to walk in His ways, and reverence Him in holy fear and communion.

Doxology
(Expression of Praise)

Now unto him that is able to keep you from falling, and to present you faultless before the presence of his glory with exceeding joy. To the only wise God our Savior, be glory and majesty, dominion and power, both now and forever. Amen. **Jude 24-25.**

Made in the USA
Columbia, SC
01 June 2022